HAL•LEONARD
INSTRUMENTAL
PLAY-ALONG

AUDIO
ACCESS
INCLUDED

PLAYBACK+
Speed • Pitch • Balance • Loop

CELLO

THE BEATLES

Cover Photo: Fiona Adams/Getty

To access audio visit:
www.halleonard.com/mylibrary

8589-2883-7332-0027

Audio Arrangements by Peter Deneff

ISBN 978-1-4950-9075-2

HAL•LEONARD®
7777 W. BLUEMOUND RD. P.O. BOX 13819 MILWAUKEE, WI 53213

In Australia Contact:
Hal Leonard Australia Pty. Ltd.
4 Lentara Court
Cheltenham, Victoria, 3192 Australia
Email: ausadmin@halleonard.com.au

Visit Hal Leonard Online at
www.halleonard.com

ALL YOU NEED IS LOVE

CELLO

Words and Music by JOHN LENNON
and PAUL McCARTNEY

BLACKBIRD

CELLO

Words and Music by JOHN LENNON
and PAUL McCARTNEY

DAY TRIPPER

CELLO

Words and Music by JOHN LENNON
and PAUL McCARTNEY

ELEANOR RIGBY

CELLO

Words and Music by JOHN LENNON
and PAUL McCARTNEY

GET BACK

CELLO

Words and Music by JOHN LENNON
and PAUL McCARTNEY

HERE, THERE AND EVERYWHERE

CELLO

Words and Music by JOHN LENNON
and PAUL McCARTNEY

HEY JUDE

CELLO

Words and Music by JOHN LENNON
and PAUL McCARTNEY

I WILL

Words and Music by JOHN LENNON
and PAUL McCARTNEY

CELLO

LET IT BE

CELLO

Words and Music by JOHN LENNON
and PAUL McCARTNEY

LUCY IN THE SKY WITH DIAMONDS

CELLO

Words and Music by JOHN LENNON
and PAUL McCARTNEY

OB-LA-DI, OB-LA-DA

CELLO

Words and Music by JOHN LENNON
and PAUL McCARTNEY

PENNY LANE

CELLO

Words and Music by JOHN LENNON
and PAUL McCARTNEY

SOMETHING

CELLO

Words and Music by
GEORGE HARRISON

TICKET TO RIDE

CELLO

Words and Music by JOHN LENNON
and PAUL McCARTNEY

YESTERDAY

CELLO

Words and Music by JOHN LENNON
and PAUL McCARTNEY